Shattered!

Hailstorm Fury

Bill Condon

MW01517801

Shattered! Hailstorm Fury

Pearson Australia
(a division of Pearson Australia Group Pty Ltd)
20 Thackray Road, Port Melbourne, Victoria 3207
PO Box 460, Port Melbourne, Victoria 3207
www.pearson.com.au

Offices in Sydney, Melbourne, Brisbane, Perth, Adelaide
and associated companies, branches and representatives throughout the world.

Copyright © Pearson Australia 2010
(a division of Pearson Australia Group Pty Ltd)

2014 2013 2012 2011
10 9 8 7 6 5

All rights reserved. No part of this publication may be reproduced,
stored in a retrieval system or transmitted in any form or by any
means whatsoever without the prior permission of the copyright
owner. Apply in writing to the publishers.

Text by Bill Condon
Edited by Eliza Collins
Designed by Cristina Neri
Illustrated by Lewis Chandler, Ficope Graphics
Photographic research by Jan Calderwood

Film supplied by Type Scan, Adelaide
Printed in China (SWTC/05)

National Library of Australia
ISBN 978 0 7312 3276 5

Acknowledgments: The author and publisher would like to thank the following for granting their
permission to reproduce copyright material:

Photographs: AAP p. 8; Australian Picture Library/J. Carnemolla pp. 9, 16, 24 left, 29 both;
Australian Picture Library/Andrew Gregory p. 31 top; Australian Picture Library/Jonathan Marks p.
27; Coo-ee Pictures p. 14; Malcolm Cross pp. 28, 29 background; Fairfax Photo Library pp. 6, 10,
26; *Newcastle Herald* p. 13 bottom; News Limited pp. 4, 25; PhotoDisc pp. 2, 7, 12, 22, 23, 30, 31
bottom; photolibrary.com/Neil Duncan p. 13 top; photolibrary.com/Cynthia Gaden p. 24 bottom
right; photolibrary.com/Geoff Higgins p. 24 top, centre right.

Every effort has been made to trace and acknowledge copyright material. The author and publisher
would welcome any information from people who believe they own copyright material in this book.

Contents

What Causes Hailstones?

Inside the tall **cumulonimbus** clouds of a big storm, the temperature at the top of the cloud is often below freezing. At the bottom of the cloud, it is warmer. Air currents in the clouds, which are called **updrafts** and **downdrafts**, are very strong. Raindrops that form in the cloud may be tossed up and down by these air currents. The raindrops freeze as they are carried up to the top of the cloud, then thaw as they drop down and meet the warmer air. This may happen several times, and each time, the raindrop gets bigger and heavier.

The **transformation** of these droplets to ice crystals requires a temperature below zero degrees Celsius, as well as tiny particles of solid matter, such as dust.

When the raindrop eventually becomes so heavy that it falls out of the cloud, it may be as a large lump of ice called a hailstone. According to scientists, an icy **conglomeration** is called a hailstone when it reaches a diameter of five millimetres. In all its forms, hail usually occurs in short spurts rather than as steady **precipitation**.

Hailstones are arranged in layers. If a hailstone is cut open before it melts, it looks like the inside of an onion. Hailstones can be as large as twelve-and-a-half centimetres in diameter. They can destroy crops, damage buildings, dent cars and kill small birds, and, occasionally, people.

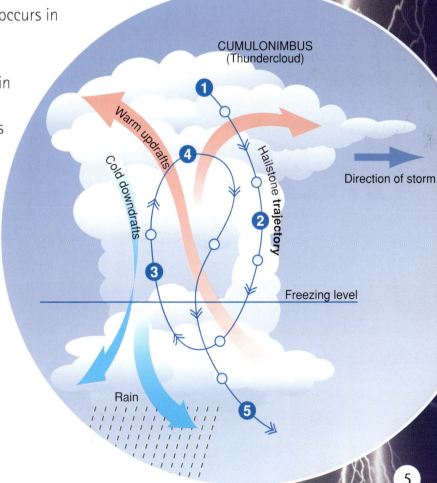

CUMULONIMBUS (Thundercloud)

Warm updrafts

Cold downdrafts

Hailstone trajectory

Direction of storm

Freezing level

Rain

1 2 3 4 5

Hailstorm Facts and Figures

Here are some are some interesting facts and figures that you probably did not know about hailstorms.

THE GREATEST TOLL

Generally, very few people are killed or injured by hailstones; for example, in Canada, where hailstorms are responsible for more than $200 million dollars worth of damage each year, there has never been a **fatality**. However, in India, in 1888, a hailstorm is said to have caused 246 deaths.

THE LARGEST HAILSTONE

Weather folklore is full of accounts of suspiciously large hailstones. Some hailstones have been described as the size of an elephant. Of course, this is an exaggeration. However, if you are hit by a large hailstone, it might feel elephant sized! The largest hailstone reported and accepted by United States Weather Bureau officials fell at Coffeyville, Kansas, on 3 September 1970. Weighing in at 758 grams, the hailstone measured forty-four centimetres in circumference.

THE LONGEST HAILSTORM

A massive hailstorm that hit Nodaway County, in the United States of America, on 5 September 1898, left hail on the ground for fifty-two days. Ice-clogged fields remained unworkable for two weeks, bringing the small farming community to a halt.

STRANGE, BUT TRUE

In 1894, a turtle encased in ice fell to the ground during a hailstorm in the Mississippi region of the United States of America.

Extraordinary Reports

This excerpt from the *Monthly Weather Review* describes the hailstorm that hit the rural town of Dubuque, in the United States of America, on 16 June 1882. Once the hailstones melted, some strange discoveries were made.

For thirteen minutes, commencing at 2.45 p.m., the largest and most destructive hailstones ever seen fell at this place. The hailstones measured from two-and-a-half to forty-three centimetres in circumference, the largest weighing over 700 grams.

Washington Park was literally covered with hailstones as large as lemons. They exhibited diverse and peculiar formations, some being covered with knobs and icicles one-and-a-half centimetres in length; others were surrounded by rings of different coloured ice with gravel and blades of grass embedded in them.

The foreman of the Novelty Iron Works, of this city, states that small living frogs were found in two large hailstones.

Denver, a city in the United States of America, has experienced two very large hailstorms in recent times. The first, on 13 June 1984, lasted a long time for a hailstorm—from 1.30 p.m. to 5.30 p.m.— as the *Storm Data Journal* reported.

The worst hailstorm in the USA ever: Denver is faced with a huge clean-up bill.

The worst hailstorm ever experienced in the Denver area in terms of damage battered the region for several hours.

Homes and other buildings sustained nearly US$200 million worth of damage. Many thousands of cars were battered by giant hailstones, and the total damage to vehicles was estimated at US$100 million.

In some areas, golfball-to-baseball-size hail fell continuously for thirty to forty minutes; some spots were pelted with a few stones as large as grapefruits. Roofs on thousands of structures were severely damaged. Innumerable car windshields were broken; two-thirds of Armada's police cars were rendered inoperable.

This 1984 storm was surpassed six years later on 11 July 1990 by a storm that hit Denver, which caused US$600 million worth of damage.

On 14 April 1999, the most violent and costly hailstorm ever was recorded in Sydney, Australia. The devastation of this hailstorm created news around the world. The damage inflicted on this Eastern seaboard city cost over A$1 **billion**.

The Sydney Hailstorm

The hailstorm that hit Sydney on 14 April 1999 struck violently and unexpectedly, leaving a trail of devastation in its wake. It was calculated that more than 500 000 tonnes of hail fell over an area of 2500 square kilometres. The next day, newspaper headlines told of an estimated $300 million worth of damage. But, later, as the storm's fury was assessed in detail, it became apparent that the damage bill was much greater. The total of the final damage bill was more than $1 billion. Miraculously, only one person was killed as a result of the storm.

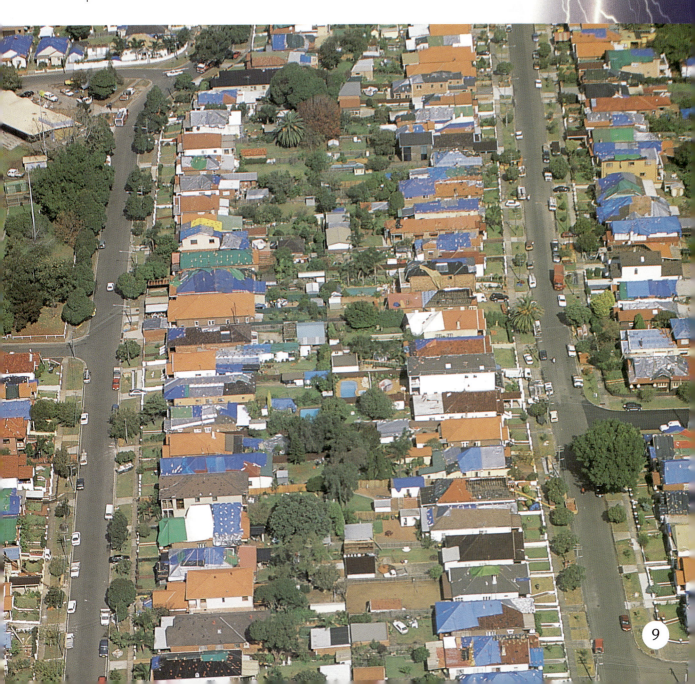

The Daily Herald

Your local newspaper—keeping you in touch daily

Thursday, 15 April 1999

80 cents

Sydney Hit by Severe Hailstorm

One man was killed as a freak hailstorm lashed Sydney last night, causing millions of dollars worth of damage.

The storm was first detected near Wollongong, in Sydney's south, at about 6.45 p.m. Pushed north by twenty to twenty-five knot winds, it hit the eastern suburbs around 7.30 p.m.

Police have confirmed that a forty-five-year-old fisherman was killed when his aluminium boat was struck by lightning.

Dozens of people were hurt. Many were hit by hailstones or by broken glass. Others were injured as they tried to repair their properties. In one case, a sixty-year-old man received severe head injuries after falling three metres from the roof of his house on to a concrete path.

Many homes lost roofs, ceilings and windows, with a number of homes so badly damaged that residents have been forced to seek alternative accommodation.

Power was cut to as many as 15 000 homes.

At Sydney's Kingsford-Smith Airport, flights were cancelled because many planes were extensively damaged.

Peter Appleton, who lives at Randwick in Sydney's east, said he has never a seen a storm so severe.

"Some of the hailstones were half the size of a man's fist," he said. "They were like hand grenades exploding on to people's roofs and smashing tiles. It was very frightening."

The State Emergency Service (SES) has received more than 4000 calls for help.

Randolph Metcalfe, one of 500 SES **volunteers**, warned that clean-up operations may continue for weeks.

"Residents with damaged homes, who are waiting for the SES to respond, should cover smashed windows with blankets and plastic," he said.

Mr Metcalfe advised people not to secure their own roofs with **tarpaulins**.

"It can be dangerous if live electrical wires are exposed," he said. "Please, leave it to us—we're the experts."

The Daily Herald

Your local newspaper—keeping you in touch daily

Friday, 16 April 1999

80 cents

Ninety-Year-Old Woman Tells of Storm Horror

Kingsford resident Mrs Emily James gave the following graphic account of the storm to staff reporter Joe Brennan.

Mrs Emily James thought she was going to die on the night of the recent hailstorm.

I'm a bit hard of hearing, so the volume of the television was up pretty loud. That's probably why I didn't hear the thunder. All I know is that I'd just finished washing the dishes, which I left out on the sink to dry as I always do.

Next second, there was a terrible racket. Crash! Crash! I almost had a heart attack. The window in front of the kitchen sink was shattered. The dishes clattered on to the floor. Smashed to pieces.

The cat howled and ran for its life, and I thought to myself, Emily, this is it. You're going to die.

I didn't know what was happening. I never thought of it as being a hailstorm. I hadn't experienced anything like it for fifty years. In the Second World War, I was a nurse.

At times, we got near the fighting and you could hear the bombing in the distance. That was the noise I heard. Nothing like a storm. It sounded like a war had broken out and all the guns were firing at me!

I live alone. My daughter's always asking me to move in with her, but I've told her I'm not afraid of anything. Between you and me, though, I was afraid last night. Terrified!

Army Joins Hailstorm Clean-Up

A week after the hailstorm that lashed Sydney, the New South Wales State Government has asked the Federal Government to let the army join the clean-up operations.

Army volunteers are helping with the massive clean-up.

With rain and wind expected to sweep the city until the weekend, some 300 army tradespeople are being rushed to the worst-affected suburbs, where an estimated 3000 houses are still exposed to the elements.

As well, eight police rescue units and several ambulance teams are assisting, together with one hundred National Parks and Wildlife Service staff, and about 120 SES workers and thirty-three firefighters from interstate.

The Director General of the SES, Major-General Hori Howard, said the army personnel would concentrate on jobs, such as repairing roof **battens** and making tarpaulins semi-permanent, so they could serve as roofs for up to six months until permanent repairs could be carried out.

The official damage bill from last Wednesday night's storm is currently $840 million, making it Australia's third most costly disaster after the 1989 Newcastle earthquake and Cyclone Tracy in 1974.

The 1989 Newcastle earthquake.

Another Violent Sydney Storm

The 1999 hailstorm is not the only one to have inflicted a lot of damage on the city of Sydney.

2 January 1947

A Bad Start to the New Year

The year 1947 got off to a bad start when a violent hailstorm hit Sydney on New Year's Day.

Central Railway Station was pounded by hail. Large pieces of jagged glass from broken windows, fell on a crowd of around 1000 people. A Bexley resident said a leather suitcase he was holding over his head was hit by a seven-centimetre-thick hailstone, which tore a twenty-centimetre hole in the case. Other residents reported seeing hailstones about half the size of a house brick.

A Paddington resident said he heard a noise "like several trains" converging on the hotel where he was staying. This was followed by hailstones the size of billiard balls, which crashed against windows, shattering them.

In another incident at Lakemba, a man's cat was killed by a direct hit from a hailstone the size of a tennis ball.

Central Railway Station before the storm.

Elsewhere, residents' homes were flooded and furniture floated around the rooms.

It was predicted that the damage from the ten-minute storm would take six months to repair.

Building experts estimated that more than one million roof tiles and half a million panes of glass would be required to replace the windows smashed in factories, houses and flats.

Countdown to the Storm

14 April 1999

SYDNEY

Observatory Hill

Bundeena

N

WOLLONGONG

3.00 p.m.
The temperature peaks at a maximum of 26.2 degrees Celsius at Observatory Hill, Sydney—about two degrees above normal.

6.45 p.m.
The storm is first detected near Wollongong, a city eighty kilometres south of Sydney. Forecasters at the Bureau of **Meteorology** expect the storm to move out to the Tasman Sea as it heads north.

7.30 p.m.
A second storm cell forms suddenly over Bundeena, a suburb in Sydney's far south, and begins pounding the city with hailstones.

8.20 p.m.
The hailstorm eases, leaving a trail of destruction in its wake.

Week one

The SES receives 1500 calls on the first night; 11 500 in the first week. Five hundred SES volunteers begin work.

The supply of 10 000 tarpaulins runs out within two days.

Week two

More than 20 000 homes are found to have suffered hail damage.

The New South Wales State Government offers a $50 000 aid package to storm victims who are not covered by **insurance** or do not have other means to pay for storm damage to their properties.

More than 5000 army workers are brought in to help with the clean-up operation.

Week three

Gale-force winds and driving rain batter homes in the eastern suburbs again.

An extra 160 SES workers arrive from interstate.

Week four

The 14 April hailstorm is officially declared Australia's worst natural disaster.

Hailstorm—14 April 1999

Week five

New estimates put the hailstorm damage bill at $1.4 billion.

Week six

Police are called in to investigate numerous cases of insurance **fraud** in relation to the hailstorm.

Week seven

About 2000 damaged homes are still listed as "priority one" by the Southern Sydney Recovery Task Force.

Week eight

Aircraft damage from the hailstorm is estimated to be $95 million.

Insurers have received more than 34 000 home and contents claims, and 53 559 motor vehicle claims.

Week nine

The SES receives more than one hundred calls as high winds loosen tarpaulins.

Hail strikes Sydney's eastern suburbs again, but there are no reports of damage.

Week ten

To date, 90 000 tarpaulins have been put in place.

Twenty million roof tiles need to be replaced.

Storm Damage Sale

QUAILE'S QUALITY CARS

have more than 200 near-new vehicles at hail-damaged prices.

Sale starts at 8 a.m. tomorrow. Be early or be sorry.

All stock must go!

PHONE 1123 4567

Robert's Roofing

Licence: 45328C

Established since 1970
All tiled roof repairs

- Re-roofing
- Storm damage
- Insurance work
- Pensioner discounts
- Free quotes
- Prompt, friendly service

ALL WORK GUARANTEED

Phone **1906 2420**

SMASHED CAR? HAIL DAMAGE?

Don't let the hailstorm put a dent in your smile. Pete the Panel Beater and his staff are ready to help.

CALL NOW FOR:

- **Free quotes on repairs.**
- **Fast service.**
- **Satisfaction guaranteed.**

Forget the rest! Pete the Panel Beater will have you back on the road *fast*.

PHONE 1883 9806

NO BINS AVAILABLE?

What a load of rubbish!

FRED'S WASTE BINS are waiting for your call.
- All bin sizes available.
- All materials accepted.

DON'T GET DUMPED ON.

Call Fred now!

PHONE 1186 1807

The Unbreakable Tile

Roof Tile Sale

- **25-YEAR WARRANTY**
- **LARGE RANGE OF COLOURS**

FREE QUOTES

Put your insurance money towards really protecting your home.

DON'T ACCEPT SECOND-BEST.

Call now: 1847 2307

Feeling power-less?

Let *Mister Ed's Electrical Enterprises* put some light back into your life.

Call us for all your domestic and commercial needs, including:
- installation and repairs
- complete home or office re-wiring
- safety switches, smoke detectors
- ceiling fans, security lighting
- hot water and stove repairs.

Special seniors discount available.

Licence: BGH77792

ASK FOR EDDIE OR PAULA.

Phone 1455 2323

Magic Carpets
Pty Ltd

Quickly, Not Costly

The management and staff of Magic Carpets Pty Ltd wish to extend their heartfelt regret to the residents who have suffered as a result of the Sydney hailstorm.

Our company has offered courteous service and quality carpets to the eastern suburbs for nearly 35 years. If your carpets have been damaged by the storm, look no further than your local carpet store—Magic Carpets.

We will look after your every need promptly, and at a price to suit.

Ring 1173 6789 for immediate attention

Slim Pickings

I am disappointed with the Weather Bureau's recent poor performance. Every evening, I watch the news specifically for the weather forecast. Yet, the night before the hailstorm hit, there was not the slightest mention of the approaching wild weather.

I find this incredible!

I work hard in my garden, and I had just watched with pride as a crop of tomatoes appeared, all red and juicy and ready to pick. If I'd had a warning from the Bureau that a hailstorm was coming, I would have picked them. As there was no warning, I didn't. Now my tomatoes are ruined. There were at least two dozen of them and I didn't get to eat one.

I have calculated the total cost of my gardening efforts to be $430.45, which includes my labour ($20 per hour), plus the cost of water, snail killer, and chicken manure. I am sending this bill to the Bureau and if I don't receive the amount in full, I will write to this newspaper again to vent my anger.

J. M. Throsby
Kensington

A Bad Joke?

I read in your 21 April issue that the State Government has very "generously" given $50 000 to the uninsured victims of the hailstorm. Are they joking?

I'm no genius, but according to my calculations, that's about two dollars per home!

I challenge the politicians to come on a guided tour of my house and others in my street and then try to justify that ridiculous amount.

B. K. Singh
Paddington

School Project

Hailstorms

WHAT IS A HAILSTONE?

Hailstones are the lumps of ice that form in some storms. They are usually round. Some hailstones are the size of a pea; some are as big as a grapefruit.

Usually, hailstones form in thunderstorms between currents of rising air called "updrafts" and currents of descending air known as "downdrafts". Large hailstones form in strong updrafts. The larger the hailstone, the stronger the updraft needed to hold it up in the storm.

DAMAGE RISKS OF HAILSTORMS

Hailstorms cause an incredible amount of damage to property and crops. On 14 April 1999, the Sydney hailstorm caused over $1 billion worth of damage. Fortunately, hail rarely kills anyone. The best way to keep safe in hailstorms is to seek shelter immediately, and to avoid open areas if possible.

An In-Depth Interview

As part of her work experience at a local newspaper, student and aspiring journalist, Julie Brennan, was asked to interview Sue Beasley, one of the SES controllers overseeing the clean-up operations in Sydney. Here is the transcript of their interview.

Student: Hello? Ms Beasley?

Sue Beasley: *That's me. Are you the work experience student I was told about?*

Student: Yes, Ms Beasley. I'm Julie Brennan from the *Eastern Standard* newspaper. I'd like to ask you a few questions.

Sue Beasley: *Please, call me Sue.*

Student: Okay, Sue.

Sue Beasley: *So the editor has asked you to write an article on the hailstorm?*

Student: That's right.

Sue Beasley: *Well, I'm very busy right now, but I remember doing work experience myself once. I'll make the time for a few questions. Fire away!*

Student: Gee, thanks, Sue. Um ... I don't know where to start.

Sue Beasley: *Maybe I'll just talk for a while and then you can ask some questions. Does that sound like a good approach?*

Student: Excellent!

Sue Beasley: *Let's do it. This storm was a freak of nature. A once-in-a-hundred-years type of storm. And, boy, am I glad it doesn't happen more often! The devastation the SES crews are seeing is heartbreaking. The storm hit without any warning. One day everything is great, then—kapow! The hail literally destroyed several suburbs. I feel very sorry for the old people, in particular. It's hard for them to cope.*

Student: Why is it worse for old people?

Sue Beasley: *Well, think about it. Many elderly people have lived in their homes for fifty years or more. All their memories are there. And most of all, home is where they feel safe. Suddenly, the hailstorm blasts them out of their comfort zone. It wrecks the homes they love, destroys their photos and souvenirs. It must be like a terrible nightmare for them.*

Student: When something like this happens, do you wish you had a different job? Something easier?

Sue Beasley: *Good question! Occasionally, I have to say yes. No-one wants this kind of intense pressure. Everyone wants our help—the phones are ringing constantly—and sleep is a bit of a luxury at the moment.*

Student: So why do you do it?

Sue Beasley: *You know what? I've never really asked myself that question. You're a good interviewer!*

Student: Thanks, Sue.

Sue Beasley: *I think I do the job for the same reason that everyone else in the SES does it— because it feels good to be able to help someone. In fact, it feels wonderful!*

Student: I understand. Do you think it will take long to clean up after the storm?

Sue Beasley: *I don't know how long. It's too big a job for the SES alone. The army is going to help. Even then it might take months. Also, there's the emotional trauma that people have gone through. That might take quite a bit longer.*

Student: Okay. I think I have all the information I need, Sue. Thank you.

Sue Beasley: *One last thing. When you write the article, please mention that I am very proud of the SES volunteers. Would you do that for me, Julie?*

Student: Yes. I promise.

Students' Experiences

The Animals and Birds Suffer, Too

Danielle Roberts, Kensington

Not many people think about the poor birds and animals that suffered as a result of the hailstorm. Our family works for WIRES—the Wildlife Information and Rescue Service. When birds and animals are hurt, people bring them to us and we look after the creatures until they are well again.

A lot of the animals in Centennial Park, which is near where we live, were either killed or injured in the storm. A ranger told us that almost half of the cormorants were killed, and hundreds of flying foxes also died.

The ranger brought us some birds to look after. There is a kookaburra, two cormorants, a heron, a tawny frogmouth, a lorikeet and an egret. They were suffering from broken wings, broken legs, or concussion.

We keep the birds in cardboard boxes in the laundry where it is quite warm. A vet came one day to treat the legs of the frogmouth and the kookaburra. He gave us some special food for the birds. Usually, Mum feeds them. She used to be afraid of them, but not any more.

When the birds have recovered, we'll release them back into Centennial Park.

A kookaburra

A heron

A cormorant

A lorikeet

A Freak Storm

Jack Carta, Paddington

The first thing I knew about the hailstorm was a strange rumbling noise. It sounded like a buffalo stampede, which lasted for about a quarter of an hour. It was really spooky.

Then, the sky went all hazy and, the next thing I knew, it was hailing. My brother Paul and I ran outside. We picked up the hail and threw it at each other. It was great fun. At first, the hailstones were about the size of golf balls, then they grew to be as big as tennis balls! We had to run back inside to avoid getting hit on the head.

The storm was frightening. It seemed as though someone was shooting at the roof. We could hear tiles smashing for ages. Mum and Dad were out at a meeting—we were all alone. We tried to be brave, but we were so scared. Especially, when some hailstones went through the tiles and through the ceiling. And then all the windows in the lounge room smashed.

My bedroom window shattered, too. Rain and hail poured in and soaked the carpet. We had to wait three days before the SES could come to put a tarpaulin on the roof. We stayed at my aunt's house because it was not safe at home.

Now, Dad has found out that we are not covered by insurance. It is going to cost him a fortune to pay for the repairs.

25

At Least We're Alive

Chris Ryland, Randwick

My street looks like a cyclone has been through it. The radio said our suburb experienced the worst of the hailstorm. During the storm, Mum, my sister and I were running around in a panic, not knowing what to do. It felt as though we were trapped in the middle of a war zone.

The ceiling in Mum and Dad's bedroom collapsed, but we escaped without a scratch. We cannot live here for a while because the house was severely damaged. We are staying with some friends in an apartment as we wait to find out what is going to happen. It is pretty crowded here, but I am not complaining.

When the hail started to fall, Dad was driving near Sydney Airport. He went into the tunnel underneath the main roadway, parked at the side of the road and waited until the worst of the storm was over. When he came out, he saw lots of cars that had been battered. They had dents all over them.

The radio said a man in an aluminium boat was struck by lightning during the storm and died. That is why I'm not complaining about anything. At least, no-one in my family was fatally injured.

A close-up photograph of Dad's damaged car.

Greetings from Sydney

Dear Auntie Di,

Did you see the reports about the Sydney hailstorm on TV?

The storm was frightening. The hailstones were as big as oranges. Our roof was damaged, and Dad's vegie patch was shredded. Also, all our windows were smashed and the carpet was drenched.

Luckily, no-one was hurt. Phew!

Love,
Jamie

AFFIX
STAMP
HERE

16 April 1999

Dear Zoe,

Thanks for your letter. It was great to read about your many adventures in England. Sounds cool! I can hardly wait for you to come home next month. I've got so much to tell you — but this next bit of news can't wait!

It all started with my dog Mintie. Two days ago, he started to howl and we didn't know why. Then, there was this strange noise like someone throwing pebbles on the roof. At first, I thought it was the naughty children next door, who like to tease Mintie.

The noise got louder and louder, so we ran outside. All we could see was the ground covered with hail. It looked like snow. Some hailstones were as big as Dad's hand; other stones were smaller. Mum ran to put the car under cover — it already had a few little dents. We had to get back inside fast because the hail was hitting us so hard that it hurt. The storm didn't last long — about twenty minutes — but it sure made a big mess.

Our street was littered with branches and uprooted trees. Some houses had gaping holes in the roof; others had smashed windows. Lots of cars had dents in them; a few had smashed windscreens. In our house, there were three broken windows and big puddles of water everywhere. We didn't have electricity for ages. My computer was on when the storm hit, so I lost everything on the screen. (Two hours worth of homework — groan!)

This week, people from the State Emergency Service have been covering damaged roof with "tarps" (that is, tarpaulins if you didn't know). The weather is still crazy—it hasn't stopped raining. If we get more hail, I'll freak!

Someone said it was the worst hailstorm to hit Sydney in 100 years. And, at school, we learnt that the hailstorm was on the anniversary of the sinking of the "Titanic"—14 April. Obviously, a bad date for disasters. Amazing, huh?

Please write back soon.

Your friend,
Ashley

Hail left after the storm.

April 15

Last night, we had a storm— a hailstorm. In our suburb, the hailstones were only about the size of marbles. Just my luck to miss the big ones. On the news, we saw hailstones as big as cricket balls!

April 16

Dad has been called away with his SES mates to help storm victims in the suburbs of Kingsford and Kensington. He came home early this morning for a few hours' sleep, then went back again. He was exhausted.

April 17

I've been helping Mum and her Red Cross friends make sandwiches and cakes for the SES workers. We made piles and piles of food. I've eaten so many sandwiches that I think I'm ready to burst.

April 18

We've hardly seen Dad since the storm started. Mum isn't very happy about it, but she understands. Dad said he and his crew have had to put up dozens of "tarps" on houses with damaged roofs. Mum told me she's worried that Dad might fall off someone's roof. I'm worried, too.

April 19

For once, I was happy to go back to school. I must have made a million sandwiches over the weekend! Dad is still working for the SES. Mum says a lot of families can not live in their homes because the storm wrecked them. I'm so glad our house is okay, but I wish Dad would come home. I guess that's selfish of me, but still …

Dad putting up "tarps".

After the storm.

Glossary

batten   a long flat strip of squared timber or metal used especially to hold something—for example, tarpaulins—in place

billion   a thousand million

conglomeration   a number of things gathered into a rounded mass

cumulonimbus   storm clouds, which look like tall black towers, that produce thunder and lightning; also known as "thunderclouds"

downdrafts   currents of descending air

fatality   an accident or disaster resulting in death

fraud   the use of false representations to gain an unjust advantage

insurance   a sum of money paid out as compensation for theft, damage or loss, and so on

meteorology   the study of the Earth's atmosphere, or air, especially to forecast the weather

precipitation   moisture that falls from the atmosphere, such as rain

tarpaulin   a heavy-duty waterproof cloth usually made from canvas

trajectory   the curved path of an object moving in air or space

transformation   the process of changing from one state to another

updrafts   currents of rising air

volunteer   a person who willingly offers their services and/or skills to help others